TO: Mackenzie,

*Shall we always remember, we conquer those with an understanding spirit of love and forgiveness.*

*- Emily J. Caldwell*

# Surmountable

## EMILY J. CALDWELL

Sold by Amazon

# CONTENTS

# FORWARD

Poetry brings us comfort as we continue to lift our hearts and rejuvenate our faith. We believe in humanity. Our understanding speaks out in our hearts with every line that is written in this book.

My journey into poetry explores the adventure of healing mentally and spiritually. During times of change in life there may be sadness or suffering. But take heart, we find encouragement in difficult times. We find the strength to help us to accept the pain that we feel in order to have growth in our life.

Good poetry speaks great truths in a universal language that can be understood by despite cultural differences. Hopefully we can find in our hearts wisdom, the force that helps us to release thoughts of the past that no longer serve us, as they are not in our new found existence.

Hopefully my book of poetry will bring to you a delightful awareness that is uplifting and fulfilling, that it will bring your mind and spirit peace, for poetry is, itself, wonderful. It is my wish that my poems will demonstrate how to Surmount the odds by believing in oneself and trusting in a universal source that is much higher than ourselves. It is for us to realize that we must be brave and courageous in being our true selves in a world that sometimes seems like it doesn't care.

*There are many ways to find Truth in Life, a truth that relates to the love of self and maintaining love for other people. When it seems impossible to feel love, know that our path in life may not be the same as one another. It is in our journey through life that our self-discovery in love grows. This challenge makes us who we are. We become people who are open and compassionate. We see the world around us change before our eyes with this new discovery of our true divine selves. We need to have a strong heart of courage and a mind of wisdom to guide us to our final destiny. We know within ourselves what we have accomplished and what we have achieved. What once was difficult has now become Surmountable!*

# I. THE BEGINNING

# SURMOUNTABLE

## BEGINNINGS

"Whatever we do has a beginning."
Beginning of love, the smiles,
The warmth in touching.
Yes, the beginning of love is quite exciting.
Precious memories that we keep in our hearts.
Yes, beginnings are so very easily to start.
But finishing the race of love by staying together
Is the hardest part!

## A NEW HEART

Feelings of my heart,
Thoughts of my mind,
Release the Illusions of my past.

They once were, but now they need to be forgotten.
Yesterday with its pain has faded away
To be lost and forgotten.

Looking up glaring at the sun,
It gives its gem of light.
It always gives its warmth.
Life comes from this light.

Yes, loving thoughts are what I am thinking,
Replacing the sadness that I once knew.
They are rolling, releasing in the wind.

Now new thoughts and feelings are finally soaring.
Making themselves known,
New thoughts of happiness. Give my heart new hope.

Yes, I can see that my future is better than my past.
I have found strength to believe,
That from many tears of sorrow,
I have grown A New Heart that's filled with Joy!

## THE GLORY

This knife wounds me so very deeply.
Making sure that my heart fills with 'The Glory!

My soul calls out with an eerie sound,
"Master, this pain I can't endure."
Tears, The Glory from my heart, Heal my soul,
For my tears are the loving prize.

Why must I feel this sorrow?
He who is greater has paid the price.
The world not I forget his sacrifice.
My Master is my constant companion.
Still my heart must become empty,
Before it can be filled with Joy of The Glory!

My spirit soars to make its freedom.
I am not in hell!
Freedom is mine!
Another cry goes out,
"Hear me Father, you are my Master,
Let your Will be done!"

I believe in your Promise,
Thy Kingdom come on earth
As it is in heaven.
I ask you for this Light.
The Victory is what I was told to believe in.
I claim it as mine today!

EMILY J. CALDWELL

*So I kneel with bended knees,*
*Speaking to a phantom,*
*A source called "God."*
*When will you appear?*
*He said, Trust Me."*
*I said, "Forgive me, I must fully believe."*

*So my Creator smiled at me,*
*Speaking, "Your tears of love mean so much to Me.*
*Tears of your heart show Me*
*Not all are chosen, only a chosen few.*
*Your tears are evidence to Me,*
*That you will receive The Glory!"*

## HEALING MY HEART

My love, without you in my life
All my days were clouds of grey.
Memories of pain would not go away.
Happiness in my life took a holiday.

My love, now here you are Healing My Heart!
With a love that is true in every way, every day.
Your sweet love is a gentle love.
It's Healing My Heart!

My love, on bended knees,
Destiny must have heard my plea.
Bring your sweet love to me.
I needed someone to call my own.
In this world, I felt so alone.

My love, loneliness wasn't my fate.
You are my knight in shining armor.
You are my man of the hour.
To me your love is like a beautiful flower,
Filling my heart with true happiness!
My broken heart has mended.
Now, it can feel love again!
Your sweet love that is gentle is Healing My Heart!

## LISTEN TO ME

It is so hard for me to do.
I am trying to reach out to you.
I want to talk with you.
But I cannot reach you.
The wound in my heart is too deep!

I am trying desperately
To express my thoughts to you.
My heart is fearful.
Like a toddler trying
To take its first step.
I am trying!

I am trying-can't you see?
I need to talk with you.
I am pleading, my heart is bleeding.
I need to talk to you!

Entangled, trapped in worldly cares,
Can't you feel me?
My love is calling, reaching out to you.
My heart needs your touch!

## SURMOUNTABLE

*Through my blinding tears,*
*You finally noticed!*
*Turning toward me,*
*You took my hand.*
*Suddenly*
*All my fears have disappeared!*
*Now, you Listen To Me!*

## COURAGE TO CONQUER

Listening to my soul,
Feeling the beating of my heart,
That lets me know that I am alive.
And that this world is mine!

Gazing outward and looking just for a moment,
Releasing, freeing the chains of my thoughts.
Making the escape to the awaiting Universe.
Having Courage as one of my resources.
My Courage is the invisible force that raises me above
Every dark beginning.

Fear is the monster I behold on their sadden faces.
I realize that now they have been caught.
Their souls are drifting in an endless pit,
Looking out staring at their gloomy cages called their
home.
They wait for their life to end and not for life to begin.

Now my thoughts escape to a happier place.
So that my mind and heart can keep their joyful
existence.
Life is not the beast that man has to Conquer.
The beast is the sword of their foolish Pride,
Their illusion of Deceit!

# SURMOUNTABLE

*Some people may think that they have won the war.*
*But I doubt this victory.*
*Their faces speak like they are their own prisoner.*
*In the darkness of their heart without light,*
*They have become a walking shadow.*
*They have no Courage To Conquer their foolish Pride*
*They have become the Illusion of Unreality!*

## THE BATTLE OF MY HEART

Yes, I am listening to you my sensitive heart,
How many times I have tried to toss you aside.
Yes, my fragile heart,
You give me love
Yet you bring me unhappy tears.
Fearing that you my heart will never mend.

Tears and more tears I have shed because of you.
Yet you still want to be
Unselfish in your giving.
Yes, my fragile heart,
Blind your eyes and close your ears
To all mediocrity.

Surely no one must know
That I keep you hidden inside of me.
You shall not be found.
Yes, my gentle heart,
You are my life for living.
You are my invisible self.
I know that love has not died inside of me

Yes, my precious heart,
It's time for you to mend,
From many wounds of sadness,
That you have felt with sorrow.
Yet my loving heart,
You still insist on unselfish giving.
I ask you my sensitive heart to forgive me.

# SURMOUNTABLE

*Take courage my precious heart,*
*And rescue your emotion of love*
*That want to live inside of me.*
*For you my sensitive heart*
*Need to be touched by another gentle heart.*
*So that the pain from my wounded heart*
*Can mend and love once again.*

## LOVE'S EYES

Love's Eyes are a ray of light
In her crystal pupils.
Her coal black eyes are infinite as a tunnel,
Which leads to the sea of knowledge.
Her smile shines like the image of a True Love Goddess.
She is of the spirit called Beauty.

Love's Eyes summon a desire
To devour lusty passions of darkness,
From the sparks of her Ultimate Light
She beans her light to all of God's creation.

Love's Eyes came to me as a stranger,
In my torrid desert
Thorny bushes and grey skies
Were in the dying world of my heart.
She found me staggering, dehydrated and screaming,
For the soothing waters,
That once flowed in my majestic soul.

Love's Eyes offered me their knowledge to energize my
will,
To slice darkness from the bond of my sovereign space.
She a conductor of Light,
That shines through my darkness for her examination.
A spark from the Ultimate Light,
Beams her light to all God's creation.
Yes, Love's Eyes fill me with your Light!

# SURMOUNTABLE

*Love's Eyes orchestrate a symphony of Holy ideas,*
*Of loving thoughts.*
*She is a seed of Life,*
*That came from that tempting fruit,*
*Once placed in Adam's hand.*
*She came to undo what had been done.*
*For no shame flows from the Holy eyes of Love.*
*Her mission is to seek Light in a Darkened world.*
*Surely Love's Eyes, I will reap your Light of Love,*
*For Eternal Life is a promise for those who believe.*

# II. THE CALL OF TRUTH

## THE MASTER CALL

*Living as one on the Earth,*
*I lived like a child of the Universe,*
*Enjoying each day to the fullest,*
*Absorbing words of Wisdom and Truth*
*That made my spirit soar.*
*I became aware, as my Heavenly Father spoke to me,*
*My precious beloved daughter,*
*Return to the Earth.*
*Help others to live, and to grow,*
*In Oneness and Unity."*

## THE HEART OF GOLD

This graceful grail that holds the brilliance of Beauty,
Shows itself with lovely thoughts
In the form of a beautiful smile.
Beauty is a kind gesture toward all mankind.
The world sees Beauty as a precious treasure.

Beauty with its gentleness hides in forgiveness.
Hoping never to surrender.
This rainbow must not let its color fade.
Knowing of the darkness that hides
In the cloud of a human's angry heart.

Listen to Beauty when it speaks,
For Beauty tears tell of a wounded heart.
Behold it!
Beauty penetrates the soul.
Beauty is a frail loving creature.
Beauty demands of itself!
It pays the price!
Beauty is the source that cries,
"I must give in order to live."

# SURMOUNTABLE

## THE POWER

On mountain tops,
Across the seas,
When I speak to strangers on the street.
I can see The Power!

We are all one.
Even though we don't look like each other.
Unity will keep this Kingdom from coming down.
I can see The Power!

If you play,
You must obey!
From the beginning,
It isn't easy.
It all depends on love.
That's all we have to believe and trust in.
I can see The Power!

But I have learned,
The Power is like the wings
Of an eagle that soars.
Nothing is Insurmountable!
We are invincible!
I can see The Power!

*At the end,*
*The Master calls.*
*The Light does not go out.*
*I can see clearly,*
*That having this Light is my victory!*
*Forever, I can see the glory!*
*I can see The Power!*

## LIFE TO THE FULLEST

Tell me what this crazy world is all about.
Just when I think I know,
I find out that I really don't.
Listening to all types of strange people.
"Why do you want to insult me?
But that's okay, I understand."
Looking at you saying one thing
And meaning something else.

This world is large enough for us to share.
Who are you to try and change my world
To look like yours?
Tell me, who are you?
Someone who thinks that you have power,
A self-made god?
Don't you know that every one's world
Is made of their own thoughts and opinions?

Years have gone swiftly by.
And here you are still trying to control me.
Tell me, who are you?
Fools, I can see your two-sided faces.
Stop it you clutter my light,
Making it harder for me to do what is right!

Strength is my shield if I must fight!
For Truth is my light, my constant companion.
And Truth helps me to seek
The secret treasure that I hope to find.

Surely, I can trod step-by-step in my mind,
And discover the hidden secret of paradise
That I hope to find.
It is covered by years of others deceitful thoughts.
Yes, it is for me alone to find this unknown world of
paradise,
And make it known to myself that I have found Wisdom.

Therefore at the end of this realm,
I will know that I have found myself in paradise knowing
Wisdom.
It is a place well-known called Life,
Which has always been here just waiting for me to
discover it,
From time and years getting to know myself!

## RED REBEL BLUE

I am known as Wolfgang,
King of the human beast. My domain is the East.
I am society's renegade.
My position is always known,
I am Red Rebel Blue!

I have had enough,
Enough of society's deceit!
Red Rebel Blue helped me to see
That I live my life being true to me!
Go ahead say what you please.
I know what is good for me!

I am Wolfgang anarchy in the flesh.
I put this world to the test!
I am a walking Armageddon!
I know the Truth!
My life code is living by one book!

I know the Truth,
That no one can rule another's soul.
Everyone is born free!
No one will take my freedom from me!
I am Red Rebel Blue!

*I am Wolfgang.*
*I have found my path in life.*
*I know me!*
*I am not a puppet!*
*This is my life's conquest!*
*I am keeping my freedom in life.*
*I call this my quest!*
*I am Red Rebel Blue!*

# DOWN TO EARTH/HEAD IN A CLOUD

To me Life was a big jigsaw puzzle,
For Life depends upon where the heart and mind
are.
Down To Earth/Head In A Cloud

As a child I was told "Keep your eyes focused,
There's only one way,
And that is the right way."
But I could not accept looking down
At the plain horizon of mediocrity.
Down To Earth/Head In A Cloud

As I became older, I rebelled!
I wished that I could see the world
In a different way.
I loved to look higher to cultivate different things.
I knew many things existed beyond
That plain horizon of mediocrity.
Down To Earth/Head In A Cloud

Everything can be seen differently
When my head is held high!
I have an imagination to see things
In a different way.
I am true to myself even if some people
Think that I am a little strange.
Down To Earth/Head In A Cloud

EMILY J. CALDWELL

So old enough, I said all my goodbyes.
I ventured into a scary yet exciting world,
Taking the ups and down in Life,
Though the years, I learned to see.
When I looked down, I was in the dumps.
But when I looked up seeing the clouds,
My head was held high!
Down To  Earth/Head In A Cloud

Now I know things are good for me in Life!
Now that I know Myself!
Down To Earth/Head In A Cloud

## AN ISLAND

Looking out at the sea,
Quieting the waves that live inside of me.
Gazing out at the peaceful sky,
I see graceful birds soaring
In a vast blue sky.
Oneness is what these graceful birds
And peaceful waters are.
They are feeling oneness
With the Universe.

The air makes itself known
With a forceful breeze
Moving to and fro.
Like the birds and the sea,
They feel their freedom
That no one can cease!

Yes!
I know within my soul I am free!
I am free to love! I am free to live!
I am free to grow!
Yes!
The sea, the birds, and I remain as one,
For there is An Island flowing
Freely inside of me!

EMILY J. CALDWELL

III. FEELINGS OF LOVE

## IN LOVE

This star, a prince, a form of god.
His love is the shield
That he shed for me.
His glow speaks!
"Yes, I am yours
And you are mine."
Yes, he is the flame
That burns inside of me.
We cast our lots,
Happiness was won.

Endless time,
Our hearts claim
We must keep ourselves free,
In this world.
Here today, we live in a foreign land.

He and I must remember
The love in our hearts.
Together, we found this Life of Love.
Now, where do we go from here?
Trusting In Love, it doesn't matter.
We will stay as One forever!

## FOOLISH PRIDE

Who is right?
Who is wrong?
When it comes to love.
Our hearts are aching.
This love we are breaking.
Let us get rid of our Foolish Pride!

What must we do?
What must we say?
How can we make our pain go away?
Can we talk it out?
Let us say what is in our hearts and start anew,
Asking for forgiveness.
We will heal each other's heart.
By getting rid of our Foolish Pride!

Within our gentle hearts,
Love burns like a blaze.
We are in each other's soul.
I need you and you need me.
Without each other, we can't go on.
Life becomes an illusion,
So we can't depart.
Let us get rid of our Foolish Pride!

Holding one another, our love will find a way.
There is no more heartache.
Love will stay our guide,
Keeping our hearts from Foolish Pride!

## A GIFT OF HEALING

I ask of you, Spirit of Love,
Let me know of your sweetness?
I want you to be a part of me,
To share your Love with others.
Love me you gentle creature.
I have scars of fear not having you near.
I need you! I need you!

Maybe I am not strong enough
To share you with others.
Yet, I want you to show me how.
Spirit of Love as I wait for you,
Life waits for me.
Help me, I need you now!

Do I give to you as you give to me?
What do I give to you?
I only have my wounded heart to offer to you.
Did I hear you say,
"Give to me your pain and your sorrows."
What is this?
I thought they were mine to keep.

Oh Spirit of Love, are you saying
That you want this part of me
This Self that has been denied?
Take this suffering and sorrow from my heart.
I can't give them to you.
My suffering and sorrow have been so long a part of
me.

Oh Spirit of Love,
Your tenderness is what I need,
To make this pain go away.
Now that you, Spirit of Love, have my sorrow,
How much lighter my heart feels!

## *FULFILLMENT*

*This cup of Need is a vessel*
*Sailing to explore the depth of a man's heart.*
*It is a hunger to fill an empty soul.*
*This emotion Need searches*
*For smiles of Light,*
*A Light of Love.*

*Uncertain as it may seem,*
*Need, needs it Light to Love.*
*To seek the warmth from another's heart.*
*Need hopes to claim,*
*"This loving- gentle heart is mine. »*

*The chest of desire is finally opened.*
*Love is the treasure wanting to be discovered.*
*Need is now anchored by the touch of another.*
*Now the cup of Need is only a phantom.*

*For the spirit of Love has forced that fear*
*Of Need into an ocean-less flight.*
*Love is claiming what is left behind.*
*There is no more Need,*
*For Love has fulfilled*
*All of my spiritual Needs.*

## THIS MOMENT

Being silent at This Moment,
I want to think of him.
Thoughts of love,
Holding me close to him.
Memories of beautiful Moments,
We shared together.

These unspoken words
Are felt so deeply.
His words of tenderness cause
Sweet memories of him to linger.

I want his love
For more than a few short hours.
I am in doubt
What shall I do?
When shall I know
If he has love for me?
Is his love the same as mine?
In time, there will be an answer.

Suddenly, I know!
I will choose not to hurry.
In time,
He will let me know,
If he is truly mine.

# SURMOUNTABLE

Surely, I can be strong,
With no hesitation.
I will give my heart to him.
And I will not let him go.

My Moments of silent do not fade away.
For love of him is only a thought away.
These sweet Moments are short,
But they make my days of happiness longer.
Now, I know that I will have him near.
Hopefully, our love will be everlasting!

# IV. FRIENDSHIP

## TRUE FRIENDSHIP

My beautiful friend, how rare you are,
For you are a precious treasure.
I have searched many faces,
In plenty of places,
To find that special person.

Who could say "I am not afraid, this is me!
Yes, I have my own unhappy fears."
True Friendship as we all know
Is what everyone wants to keep
In their soul.

So thank you my True Friend
For accepting me
Just as I am.
Because I am not
What I sometimes appear to be.

I am sure that in time
We may depart.
But happy memories of laughter,
And tears of joy will always be remembered.

So my True Friend,
May we trust to know,
That the love we discovered together,
As True Friends,
Will live as we grow.

## WHO AM I?

May I tell you Who I Am?
I am a person sensitive to love and pain.
So why do I pretend?
Shall I say what is within my loving heart,
That I would like to share,
Knowing that I have nothing to fear?

May I tell you all my precious dreams
And my inward thoughts?
Because I have searched and found out
What this world is all about.
I am sure you will find out
Who I Am.
Why, I Am just another You!

## AS ONE

When we spoke our inward thoughts,
Our longing and loving hearts became As One.
Unknowing at our first glance,
Our caring love could make the two of us
Stand As One.

For sharing of loving hearts and happy souls,
Made the two of us become As One.
Because we have Understanding and Forgiveness
In our hearts,
We shall always remain As One!

## JUST LIKE ME

Ageless, so I don't remember,
When giving thoughts created my being.
I reach out to touch another's heart.
But my caring thoughts were unknown,
Because of the fear in another's heart.

How long must I conceal these tears?
Tears of wanting to be touched and understood.
There are many shades of my thoughts
That live inside of me.

After years of searching,
Lifetimes wasted away.
At Last!
I have found another tender heart!
Just Like Me!

## ECHO

Doves and sparrows with their playful grace,
Dragons with their fire breath,
They all try to live as one.

The birds are wingless as minute embryos.
And dragons draw breath
For their new hopeful flight.
All together they are "breaking free"
And climbing to the light.
Cries of their voices can be heard-
"We too need to be touched
For our flight to the light."

The sound that the birds make
Creates a truth that echoes
Like the birds and dragons.
Listening to their Echo of true being,
I now realize there is much to learn.

How man can learn to live in Unity,
For there are higher mountains to climb in
Humanity.
Oneness is an Echo always waiting for us
To surrender our Will
For a greater Whole.

# *V. DETERMINATION*

## MY DISCOVERY

Why do illusions appear as if they are real?
Surely there is an answer to every question.
Where shall I begin?
What shall I take on this exciting
Journey that I must travel?

What an adventure
Traveling up this lonely yet peaceful road.
My thoughts are so very new.
I see mysteries and keys to My Discovery.
I must possess these keys,
For they open my soul to Truths and Freedom!

What else am I to find
In this reservoir for My Discovery?
Here is the answer to that puzzling question.
Yes, I knew that I would find my answer.
Now I know that all my answers
Are found inside of me.

Finally, after years of searching
And joyful tears,
Happiness is what I have found.
This is amazing!
This is My Discovery.

## TAKING MY CHANCES

I am not afraid to live my Life!
This is my resolution.
To make all my dreams become a reality!
Time has taught me how to see the LIGHT!
That I am free to travel my own rainbow!
To live my Life happy and free!
That is the Life for me!
I am Taking My Chances to be a shining star!

Today, I am feeling down and out.
But I am not throwing in that towel,
Even if my tears rain down on my face.
I am a woman whose spirit is strong!
I know that I possess great possibilities!
No matter how hard Life may seem,
Life is only a dream.
I Am Taking My Chances to be a shining star!

Each day unfolds with new Hope,
To help me reach my goal.
From now on, it does not matter
What people may say about me!
Nothing is going to hold me back!
Whenever it may seem I have failed,
I will keep my Hope and try, try again.
I Am Taking My Chances to be a shining star!

## AT THE TOP

I am at The Top!
I am at The Top!
The way was not easy.
But I did not stop!
Look at me!
I finally made it,
At The Top!

Many days I felt discouraged,
But I believed in a Higher Power.
So I did not stop.
This Higher Power guided my way.
Things turned around for me.
I finally made it,
At The Top!

I am At The Top!
Some people may wonder,
How I came to be
At The Top!
With help from above,
It was meant for me!
To be, to live At The Top!
I finally made it,
At The Top!

## MAKE IT

Yes, you can do it
If you have the desire to Make It!
Today, you may feel all alone.
Your hope is almost gone.
This big world just doesn't seem to care.
But you can Make It!

Sometimes life seems like it isn't fair,
But you have to hang in there.
Don't give up.
Don't let go.
Your faith is made strong while you wait.
You will Make It someday!

The road may look long to get your pay,
But you know that you can't live any other way.
You can travel that golden rainbow.
Yes, you can Make It!

Now that you know, every move will make you a winner!
You have learned the rules of the game of life.
Now you are number one!
Everyone knows your name!
Because you have kept the faith,
You can Make It!

# SURMOUNTABLE

Looking back at my beginning
My journey in life was long and rough.
But if I had to,
I would do it all over again!
For the lessons I learned
Taught me how to be steady.
I took my greatest weakness
And made it into my gold, my treasure.
Now, no fear stands at my door.
Yes, I did Make It!

EMILY J. CALDWELL

## ALL THE WAY

Every morning it's the same old thing.
I wake up to a daring world.
I know some things never change,
Like the power of the dollar.
This is how it's meant to be,
To live in the land of the free!
So I am going All The Way!

I am going All The Way!
I know that my spirit is strong!
I am capturing all of my fears!
I just keep rolling on,
Even if some people try to give me hell!
Yeah, Yeah, Yeah

I am going All The Way!
I will not be defeated!
I am determined nothing or no one
Can stand in my way.
No one or nothing will hold me back!
I am going All The Way!

In this daring world,
My head is held high with dignity!
I am traveling across my own rainbow!
I am going to be a shining star!
I will reach my Destiny!
I am going All The Way!

# VI. INSPIRATIONAL

# SURMOUNTABLE

## MY INSPIRATION

So I want Fame and Fortune?
First I must be taught a couple of things.
Where is My Inspiration?

Looking around, I didn't know.
I was told to go forth.
I was "earth-bound."
I reached my destination,
Looking for My Inspiration.

Crazy!
This world is strange.
The Unknown keeps knocking me down.
I keep falling on my pretty little cane,
Trying to find My Inspiration.

Taking the time to sit and think,
I realize over the years,
I finally learned the clue
To My Inspiration

All I have ever needed
Was found inside of me!
Rays of light started to dance
An electrifying act inside of me.
I was surprised! I began to shout!

EMILY J. CALDWELL

*I am My own Inspiration,*
*Me, Wonderful Me!*
*Now I have My Fame and My Fortune.*
*I know that I have success*
*Growing inside of me.*
*I know I have Courage and Confidence*
*To be True to Me!*
*This is My Inspiration!*

## THE CALL OF FAITH

The Master is the existence of my being.
I am searching to know
How is He the Father?
Knowledge is the sword
That cuts through my thoughts.
Causing mankind to reap the seed of pride.

Ageless, believing in an old ancient language
Called "The Ultimate Truth."
Seeking this Truth,
Having too much pride is my enemy.
Making an emptiness,
I search deeper.

How is this Master my soul keeper?
Now, my soul cries out To this Supreme Being.
"My Lord, I want to know you as my Father."

I release thoughts and feelings
That I once thoughts were true.
Now new thoughts make me feel
Like the birth of an infant.

## EMILY J. CALDWELL

*Just as an infant want to be held,*
*Hold me Father close to you!*
*Just as a baby moves on crawling knees,*
*So I too, am on bending knees,*
*Oh Lord, I pray to you!*
*Show me your face.*
*Do I really look like you?*
*Can I live my life*
*The Way of Truth?*

SURMOUNTABLE

## SHIELD OF INNOCENCE

My new life came from a warm sober womb.
My mind was empty of worldly cares.
For my birth came from the kingdom,
The work of my heart.

Now it is said when my mind speaks to my heart
"Learn anew,
Erase the darkness within you.
Let not your heart become polluted,
And do not let hypocrisy abound,
By the legacy of a darkened world."

Let Love and Peace grow within
For these feelings are a gift to me
As an Innocent child.
My precious seed of light is mine!

I will not let this light be stolen from my Innocent
heart.
I will take Courage!
No dark cloud will bury me On my spiritual
journey.

How can they do this to me?
No! This cannot be! I claim my birthright!
I am an Innocent child!
Save Me!

EMILY J. CALDWELL

*Now my light will last*
*On my spiritual journey to eternity.*
*Darkness will not smother my Innocent heart.*
*"Don't leave me!*
*Save me from the walking dead!"*

## VAIN GLORY

Who wanders aimless like an ant,
Not keeping the laws of an invisible world called the
Universe?
Yet in time, there is departure.
Finding out a moment too late, there is no turning
back
For another chance.

Those who are lawless,
Enter into a strange dim frightened world.
Their cries of fear can only be heard,
Because they are stripped by their Pride.

Now they can see themselves looking into a mirror.
No honor, but horror is now revealed.
Their Vain Glory that was once sought,
Has turned these creatures into a pillar of salt.
There they will stay in their frightened world.
They are now lost and forgotten!

## I AM TAKING THE TIME

The Transformation of my mind and spirit,
Is like newness of a rosebud in bloom.
What was needed was Time
For me to change yesterday's ancient thoughts.
The gift of Life has brought me
'The quietness to be Free!

I need this Freedom to be just me!
I must hold on to the dreams
That live inside of me.
This is my Time to be True to me.
Sometimes, I need to have
The Time and Freedom to weep.

Soon the freshness of my mind and spirit
Will soon appear.
Like lovely fresh-picked flowers to enjoy.
So, I let go.

With this Freedom and Time,
I am like a bird,
Taking its first graceful flight
I rest both my mind and heart
To give more love
At a better Time!

## WHOLENESS

These scales called emotions must ding!
Without them I cannot go on.
The whole has many parts,
And they all have their own existence.

The depth of my heart
Is filled with a warm-like substance,
Calming the tempest which lives
Behind my jaded mask.
My thoughts move toward
This brightness of light,
Forming in this kaleidoscope
Of thought and emotions.

The eye of Truth stares with its rays,
Making the secret pattern known,
That this Self needs
The emotion called Hope,
So that it can survive.

Truth and Love show my soul
That before our birth in this world
Our hearts were created
To make Humanity.
With this togetherness,
We create the secret of Wholeness!

## ENDURANCE

I have learned that no circumstances and no
situations
Can make me stumble or crumble.
For years have passed,
And I can see,
The Light that is ahead of me.

I have found that Meekness is a Strength,
Giving me Courage and Confidence.
Now I can resist!
For I have learned and know now
Of the cold and heat of man's changing heart

New thoughts are clear in my mind.
What is the key for the rest of time?
Yes, I know, I have found Strength,
Now I know that I can Endure!

# VII. LYRICS

## MY LOVE, MY LIFE, MY REALITY

My Love, My Life, My Reality
I declare to you,
"Yesterday, today, forever,
My heart beats for you only.
I will never let you go."
You are My Love, My Life, My Reality.

My Love, whenever I am feeling down,
I think of you only.
It is you who makes my world happy again.
Our love will stand the test of time!
We will keep our love alive.
For you will always be
My Love, My Life, My Reality.

My Love you are My Life and you are My Reality.
I promise you with this solemn vow,
"You will always be mine,
And I will always be yours,
We will always love one another."
'This is our destiny,
Throughout Eternity!
You will always be
MY Love, My Life, My Reality.

## TENDER TOUCH

In your arms tonight, your Tender Touch
Says "Here is where I belong!"
You are the one I have been dreaming of.
When we are together nothing matters.
Your Tender Touch makes my heart feel
That your sweet love came from above.

Until now I never knew,
How could I ever live without you?
You are the joy my tender heart beats for,
Because of one sensation that means so much to
me,
Your warm and wonderful Tender Touch!

I am caught in your cloud of love.
It melts all of my defenses.
Pleasure of passions quickly begins,
Making my reality come to an end.
Drifting off to paradise,
Your Tender Touch makes this night stand so still.
I will not think until tomorrow.
Tonight, I have been hit by cupid's arrow.

Whisper softly in my ear
Making my joyful heart hear
"That I am in your loving soul.
Tonight is the beginning of our love,
That has made the two of us become whole."
All because of this one sensation
That means so very much to me.
Your wonderful Tender Touch!

## A WOMAN

A woman without a man
Is A Woman who weeps.
A woman is made for a man's kind of loving.
A Woman needs her man,
When she knows that she is afraid,
And she doesn't have to be the boss.
She knows how to be pleasing.

A Woman needs her man
If she is to survive!
That is how it is meant to be,
At the beginning of time,
And now that is how it's going to stay!

A Woman will let it be!
She knows whatever the reason is.
But she also knows
That she, as a Woman, was created
For a man's kind of loving!

*EMILY J. CALDWELL*

## I WANT TO MAKE SWEET LOVE TO YOU

You melt all my defenses,
Making my love come tumbling down.
Your tender love moves every inch of me.
My body quivers!
I surrender to your touch.
I have become a willing prisoner!
I Want To Make Sweet Love To You!

My dream has come true!
Here you are holding me close to you.
Now your warm embrace is my one and only fantasy.
Beneath this full moon light,
Time moves so slowly,
Like sand in an hourglass.
I don't want to think.
I only want to surrender to your touch.
I Want To Make Sweet Love To You!

My world, this fantasy has come true,
You holding me close to you!
I want this feeling to last forever!
You make my heart beat wild.
I feel like a happy child!
I Want To Make Sweet Love To You!

# SURMOUNTABLE

*Love is in the air.*
*I see happiness everywhere·*
*In the streets, on the beach.*
*I see the love that you have for me!*
*I await to hear your voice,*
*Telling me, "Woman you are mine, stay here with me.*
*I Want To Make Sweet Love To You!"*

## PLAYING WITH THE BOYS TONIGHT

I am the greatest fun in town.
All you girls gather around.
I am going to school you,
About what is going down!
Playing With The Boys Tonight

Girls, if your life seems dreary,
Always sitting home with the sisters.
Don't be leery, have some fun tonight.
Hey little sister learn my style.
Know what to say and do.
Sometimes it's good to act wild!
Playing With The Boys Tonight

Today's news isn't legendary.
A man is a grown-up boy,
Looking to play with a good-looking toy!
Men are the greatest, the best creation.
Sure, men seems stubborn like mules.
But, be no fool!
They make the rules.
Playing with the Boys Tonight

# SURMOUNTABLE

When the sun goes down,
The wolf comes out!
Men want to play with us girls.
So have some fun!
My sweet sister take my advice,
"Tease to please, be sweet like honey.
If you play it right,
He will be holding you tight!"
Have some fun!
Playing With The Boys Tonight

## LITLE MISS SENSUOUS

Hey sweet thing, what's your name?
Give to me your home number.
I will give you a time that you will remember.

Little Miss Sensuous
You are desire in motion.
Let me be the one!
Wow, Yeah! Swing those hips!
Let me be the one!
Little Miss Sensuous

How can anyone look so good?
You can turn any guy's head!
You are hot, red-hot, hot!
I can't help myself.
I want to get next to you!
Little Miss Sensuous

Girl, you can satisfy the wolf in this guy!
Let me take a big bite of you.
That mini dress sure looks good on you!
You are hot, red-hot, hot!
Let me take you home.
I will make you mine, all mine.
Little Miss Sensuous

SURMOUNTABLE

## IT'S PARTY TIME

Life is a big celebration!
The week is gone.
We have worked from nine to five.
It's time to dance those blues away.
So come alive, pass that wine.
It's Party Time!

Listen to the music.
Get down tonight
Celebrate, Celebrate, Celebrate,
Just dance, dance, dance,
It's Party Time!

You have put on your dancing shoes.
Grab your partner!
We are going to party!
That's right!
We will not stay uptight!
We are going to party!
Listen to the music.
Celebrate, Celebrate, Celebrate,
It's Party Time!

## ENTICE ME BOY

Our first kiss on our first date,
Your caress melts all of my defenses.
I see pleasure in your eyes.
Should I give into you?
What is a girl to do?
Charm and captivate my heart!
Stimulate and seduce my heart.
Entice Me Boy!

I have nothing to say.
I am feeling this hungry desire.
I can no longer resist!
Tonight, temptation has put its spell on me.
What am I to do?
Charm and captivate my heart!
Entice Me Boy!

I won't think until tomorrow,
Until the morning sunlight.
Tonight this feeling is so right
Lying here in your arms,
Reality has come to an end.
I surrender to your charm.
Now seduce my heart.
Give to me more moments of pleasure.
Tonight, I am yours!
Entice Me Boy!

## *COOL MY FIRE*

*Cool My Fire! Make me feel alive!*
*From my head down to my toes.*
*I want to feel revived!*

*Come to me my love,*
*To my fire of desire.*
*You are what I need!*
*Take me in your arms.*
*Boy don't be shy.*
*I need you!*
*To Cool My Fire!*

*This fire of desire flames with passion.*
*Too many nights I have felt this passion.*
*I can't put up a fight*
*Hush just Cool My Fire!*

*Yes, that's right!*
*Put your arms here and squeeze me tight!*
*Don't hesitate!*
*Sugar, you know how to do it right!*
*I want you to Cool My Fire!*

## EMILY J. CALDWELL

*At last, this is paradise!*
*Our passion burns out of control.*
*Yes, take me twice!*
*I am a woman not a shy little girl.*
*I love to feel pleasure,*
*Just one more time.*
*Cool My Fire!*

## ON THE PROWL

*I am tossing your picture aside.*
*Today, I learned about your lies.*
*You are a two-timing lover!*
*I am finished with you boy!*

*Girls, he's a hound On The Prowl*
*Chasing after every girl he see,*
*Getting his kicks with any chick!*
*He's no angel!*
*He's a hound On The Prowl.*

*Boy, your name will be put to shame!*
*I am sounding the alarm.*
*I am telling all my girlfriends*
*The word will spread around town.*
*He's a hound On The Prowl!*

*I remember when you walked into my life.*
*You loaded my head with your sweet lies.*
*Telling me I was your only love!*
*Boy, you had the perfect lines.*

*So before you go boy,*
*I want you to know.*
*You will never see me cry*
*For a two-timing playboy*
*Who is a hound On The Prowl!*

EMILY J. CALDWELL

## COME BACK TO ME

I have broken my lover's heart,
I am to blame.
With my foolish, selfish kind of love.
I remember the joy we once shared.
In our love affair.
These precious memories keep me lingering on.

Come Back To Me, my love.
I've tried to live without you.
Let our love be our guide.
Don't let our love die!
Come Back To Me!

There will be no more tears.
No more pain to feel what made both of us to cry.
Hurry, hurry,
Come Back To Me!

Time has come and gone.
We have been alone far too long.
But I am still waiting patiently for his return.
True love will give it one more try,
Before we say our last goodbye!
Come Back To Me!

# SURMOUNTABLE

*Now he has Come Back To Me!*
*I will show him this time*
*I really love him and that I will truly care!*
*I will be sincere!*
*Now I know that he truly loves me!*
*My love has Come Back To Me!*

# VIII. AFTERWORD

EMILY J. CALDWELL

# SURMOUNTABLE

## AFTERWORD

In our spiritual journey into Life, we want to be victorious, not defeated by situations and circumstances we encounter each day. In our quest to go inward, we find the Faith of our true being. It is for us alone to know that we are overcomers and we rise above or go beyond the negative challenges we face. It is for us to prevail in our Faith; to find our inner strength to endure the lessons that Life is trying to teach us; to have Courage and Confidence in who we are. Once we realize our divine self, we can begin to release outworn thoughts with this new awareness. This helps us to move forward in our journey within ourselves.

Our spiritual journey inward is to admit to ourselves that we do not accept what the world wants us to believe. It takes Courage to conquer our fears. It is our invisible force that rises us above every dark beginning. Fear is our enemy in Life that we conquer within ourselves. We acknowledge, either accept or reject the existence of what is Truth for our own being. Truth gives us Confidence to act not to doubt our own true selves.

*Therefore, we are able to improve our quality and character to excel and prevail over our challenging circumstances in Life. As we grow in this newfound knowledge of truth, we begin to perceive Life in a different way. We are learning Wisdom. Our Courage and Confidence have become stronger to beat the odds that we face in our inward spiritual journey into Life!*

*Now, we have done the impossible by believing in our true selves which we have found. And here in these moments of Truth, we have accepted our own individual path to live in Life. Now we can finish our spiritual journey, for all that remains is rather easy to attain. All obstacles have become defeated or removable. We have accomplished our goal! We have achieved the impossible! We now know how to overcome to conquer, to be Surmountable!*

## ABOUT THE AUTHOR

Emily Caldwell was born in Florida. She has a degree in Marketing from Indiana University, Bloomington. She has traveled extensively within the United States and is a mother of three sons. She enjoys writing poems and lyrics inspired by her life's journey.

# EMILY J. CALDWELL

Made in the USA
Middletown, DE
04 February 2019